THE
Pointless Book

STARTED BY ALFIE DEYES
FINISHED BY YOU

BLINK
bringing you closer

BLINK
bringing you closer

Published by Blink Publishing
Deepdene Lodge
Deepdene Avenue
Dorking RH5 4AT, UK

www.blinkpublishing.co.uk

facebook.com/blinkpublishing
twitter.com/blinkpublishing

978-1-905825-90-5

A CIP catalogue of this book is available from the British Library.

Designed by www.envydesign.co.uk

Printed and bound by GGP Media GmbH, Pößneck

7 9 10 8

Blink Publishing is an imprint of the Bonnier Publishing Group
www.bonnierpublishing.co.uk

THE POINTLESS BOOK APP

WATCH ALFIE IN ACTION

SCAN ME

TAKE POINTLESSNESS TO ANOTHER LEVEL WITH THE POINTLESS BOOK APP WITH EXCLUSIVE VIDEOS FROM ALFIE AND MORE! ACCESS THE FREE APP FROM ITUNES OR GOOGLE PLAY, POINT YOUR DEVICE AT THE PAGES WITH THE ICON ABOVE, AND THE VIDEOS WILL BE REVEALED ON SCREEN. HERE YOU WILL GET THE CHANCE TO WATCH VIDEOS OF ALFIE MAKING A CAKE IN A MUG, PLAYING HAND SLAPS AND TAKING PART IN THE VARIOUS HILARIOUS CHALLENGES AND ACTIVITIES!

THE POINTLESS BOOK APP REQUIRES AN INTERNET CONNECTION TO BE DOWNLOADED, AND CAN BE USED ON IPHONE, IPAD OR ANDROID DEVICES. FOR DIRECT LINKS TO DOWNLOAD THE APP AND FURTHER INFORMATION, VISIT WWW.BLINKPUBLISHING.CO.UK.

COMPLETE THIS BOOK IN A POINTLESS ORDER!

MY JOURNAL THIS WEEK

WRITE DOWN ONE SENTENCE TO DESCRIBE EACH OF YOUR DAYS THIS WEEK.

MONDAY _____

_____

TUESDAY _____

_____

WEDNESDAY _____

_____

THURSDAY _____

_____

FRIDAY _____

_____

SATURDAY _____

_____

SUNDAY _____

_____

STICK A PHOTO HERE

WRITE DOWN YOUR FAVOURITE QUOTE AND WHO SAID IT

SEE ALFIE'S QUOTE

SPRAY YOUR FAVOURITE SCENT ON THIS PAGE FOR WHEN YOU'RE FEELING DOWN

SMELL ME

WOULD YOU RATHER...

SEE ALFIE'S CHOICES

1) Have wings or fins?

2) Have sweets for dinner every day for a month or have a pint of curdled milk?

3) Have no elbows or no knees?

4) Be in a cave of spiders or snakes?

5) Swim with crocodiles or sharks?

6) Drink your own urine or eat your own vomit?

7) Fight a horse-sized duck or 100 duck-sized horses?

8) Have legs as long as your fingers or fingers as long as your legs?

9) Be sexually attracted to fruit or have Cheetos dust permanently stuck to your fingers?

10) Speak any language fluently or be able to speak to animals?

WRITE DOWN YOUR TOP FIVE CELEBRITY CRUSHES

(LOOK AT THIS LIST A MONTH FROM NOW AND SEE IF YOU STILL AGREE!)

1.

2.

3.

4.

5.

ORIGAMI TIME!

CUT OUT THIS SQUARE AND FOLLOW THE
INSTRUCTIONS ON THE NEXT PAGE

CUT HERE

CUT HERE

CUT HERE

ORIGAMI TIME!

INSTRUCTIONS:

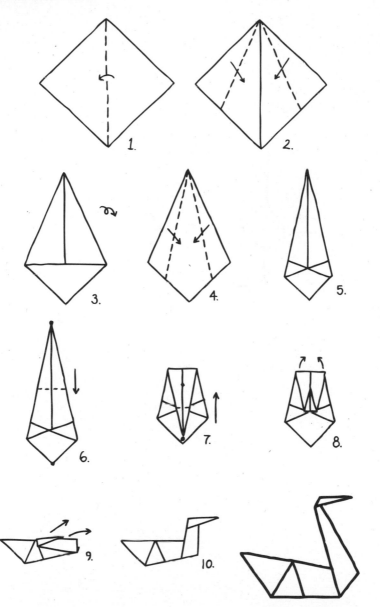

MAKE A PICTURE...

...WITH THE CIRCLE

BUCKET LIST

WRITE DOWN TEN THINGS YOU'D LIKE TO DO BEFORE YOU GET OLD...

1.

2.

3.

4.

5.

6.

7.

8.

9.

10.

TAKE YOUR POINTLESS BOOK ON A DATE...

WHERE DID YOU GO?

_____
_____
_____
_____
_____

WHAT DID YOU TALK ABOUT?

_____
_____
_____
_____

DID YOU KISS?

_____
_____
_____

ACCENTS CHALLENGE

Play the accents challenge with a few friends! Do your best impression of someone talking in the following accents and ask your friends to guess the country:

AUSTRALIAN

JAMAICAN

AMERICAN

FRENCH

CHINESE

SCOTTISH

POINTLESS
PAGE!

WHEN YOU SEE THIS PAGE FILL IT IN WITH WHATEVER YOU WANT!

DRAW THE HAIR!

DRAW THE HAT!

DRAW SOME MAKE UP...

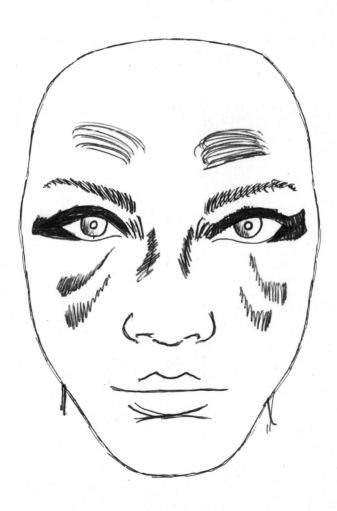

SPOT THE DIFFERENCE...

...FIVE DIFFERENCES TO FIND!

BRIGHTON PIER

BRIGHTON PIER

DREAM JOURNAL

LAST NIGHT I DREAMT: _____

_____

_____

_____

_____

_____

_____

_____

_____

_____

_____

_____

_____

_____

_____

_____

_____

_____

I THINK THIS MEANS: _____

_____

_____

_____

_____

_____

_____

WRITE A MESSAGE FOR A FRIEND AND SWAP PAGES WITH THEM...

TEAR HERE

TAKE A BITE OUT
OF THIS PAGE

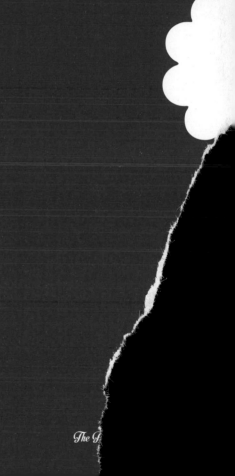

The

FAVOURITE EVER...

(LOOK BACK IN A MONTH AND UPDATE!)

BOOK: _This one!_

SONG: _happy little pill_

COLOUR: _mint_

YOUTUBER: _Zoella_

FRIEND: _Ellie_

BLOGGER: _Zoella_

VIDEO GAME: _Minecraft_

ILM: _ELF_

TE: _youtube_

Book

EAT SOME DRY CRACKERS...

HOW MANY CAN YOU GET IN YOUR
MOUTH AT ONCE?

_____

HOW FAST CAN YOU EAT ONE
CRACKER?

_____

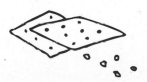

THE DICE GAME

CUT OUT THE PAPER CUBE TEMPLATE ON THE OPPOSITE PAGE, FOLD ON THE LINES AND TAPE TOGETHER TO MAKE THE DICE!

WRITE DOWN SIX THINGS THAT YOU **HAVE** TO DO IF YOU ROLL THE DICE ON THAT NUMBER. IT CAN BE A DARE, A GOOD DEED, ANYTHING, BUT YOU HAVE TO DO IT!

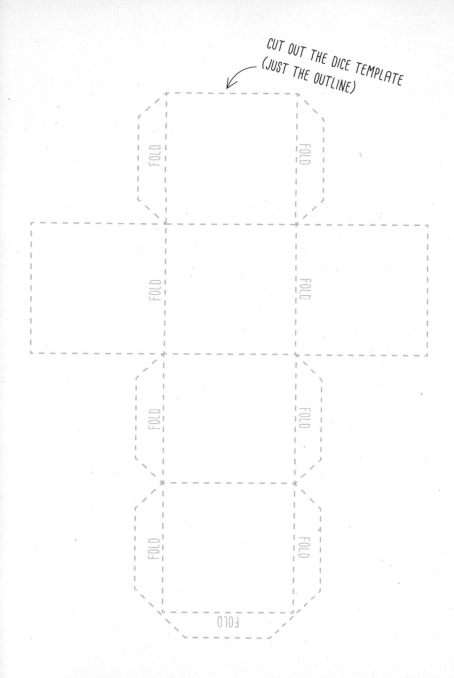

CUT OUT THE DICE TEMPLATE (JUST THE OUTLINE)

FOLD FOLD FOLD FOLD FOLD FOLD FOLD FOLD FOLD

(YOU WILL NEED STICKY TAPE!)

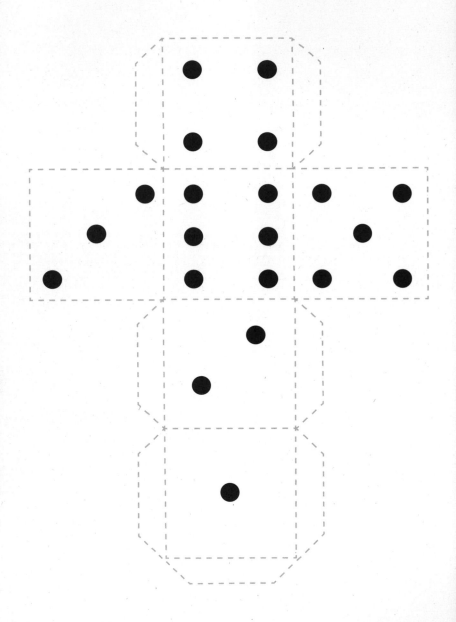

PLAY HAND-SLAPS

SCAN HERE

KEEP SCORE HERE:

PLAYER 1	PLAYER 2

WINNER: _____

DESIGN A TATTOO

DRAW A TATTOO YOU'D LOVE TO GET IN THE FUTURE

STAPLE THIS PAGE

CREATE SOME ART
#THEPOINTLESSBOOK
WITH YOUR DESIGN

PEOPLE-WATCHING PAGE...

TICK WHEN YOU SEE:

☐ A MAN WITH A BEARD

☐ A LADY WITH RED HAIR

☐ SOMEONE WEARING A CAST

☐ A CHILD WITH A DUMMY

☐ A YELLOW CAR

☐ SOMEONE TAKING A SELFIE

☐ A POSTMAN

DRAW THESE SHAPES...

...WITHOUT TAKING YOUR PEN OFF THE PAPER

CONSEQUENCES...

FOLD HERE

CONSEQUENCES...

PLAY WITH A FRIEND!

1. WRITE DOWN A GIRL'S NAME, FOLD IT OVER AND HAND TO THE NEXT PLAYER.

2. WRITE A BOY'S NAME, FOLD IT OVER AND PASS ON AGAIN.

3. WRITE WHERE THEY MET, FOLD OVER AND PASS ON.

4. WRITE WHAT SHE SAID TO HIM, FOLD OVER AND PASS ON.

5. WRITE WHAT HE SAID TO HER.

6. CONSEQUENCE...YOU DECIDE THE ENDING.

7. UNRAVEL THE STORY AND READ BACK!

WRITE DOWN YOUR FIVE FAVOURITE THINGS ABOUT YOURSELF AND WHY...

1.

2.

3.

4.

5.

PASS YOUR BOOK TO A STRANGER AND ASK THEM TO DRAW A PICTURE OF YOU...

WORD SEARCH!

B	O	Y	O	U	T	U	B	E	A	P	T	A	Q	R
F	I	R	B	V	B	T	S	X	H	C	B	C	H	P
O	N	D	V	J	R	S	E	W	P	O	H	S	G	O
T	K	J	K	G	M	K	W	N	Y	F	K	K	P	I
R	S	N	T	I	J	Y	S	D	R	F	C	V	S	N
A	M	J	L	Y	N	T	V	R	M	E	R	J	B	T
V	G	E	L	P	R	I	E	H	B	E	T	J	R	L
E	R	L	G	L	M	G	T	N	Q	Z	D	N	B	E
L	V	S	X	U	G	C	U	S	R	T	Z	K	I	S
E	D	U	T	O	W	F	B	Y	D	E	W	E	C	S
M	O	V	L	S	Z	G	T	H	I	U	L	U	F	B
L	N	V	O	P	L	H	B	R	E	F	Y	H	R	O
D	C	S	G	N	I	W	N	E	K	C	I	H	C	O
T	H	T	P	O	C	D	G	W	N	F	C	K	O	K
B	R	I	G	H	T	O	N	X	S	S	F	N	Y	S

YOUTUBE	SMILE	COFFEE
VLOGGER	BRIGHTON	INTERNET
POINTLESS BOOK	TRAVEL	CHICKEN WINGS

TRACE THE OUTLINE OF YOUR FAVOURITE FOOD ON THIS PAGE...

CONCERTINA STORY

WRITE A COUPLE OF LINES OF A STORY, FOLD BACK THE PAGE FOR A FRIEND TO
WRITE THE NEXT LINE AND SO ON... OPEN UP TO REVEAL A HILARIOUS STORY

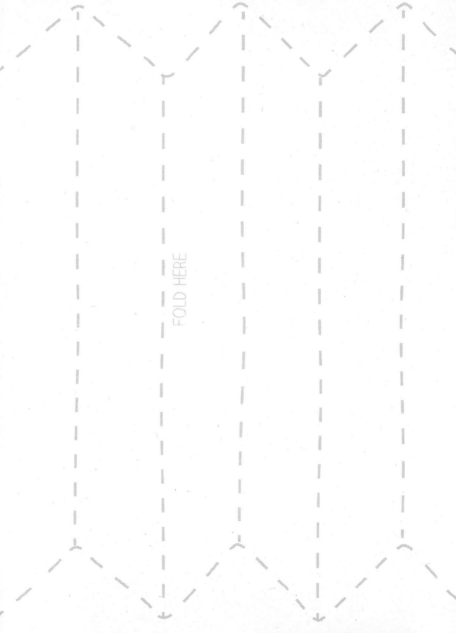

FOLD HERE

...IRON THE CREASES OUT OF THIS PAGE.

PLAY A SONG AND WRITE THE LYRICS ON THIS PAGE...

DRAW GENITALS ON THE PEOPLE BELOW...

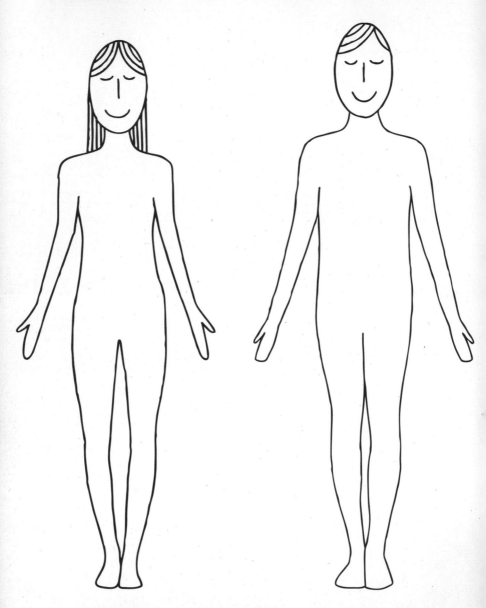

WRITE A COMPLIMENT ON
THIS PAGE, RIP IT OUT
AND PASS IT TO A FRIEND

TAKE A PHOTO OF YOURSELF HOLDING YOUR
BOOK IN THE CRAZIEST PLACE YOU CAN
THINK OF AND UPLOAD IT USING

#THEPOINTLESSBOOK

MAKE THIS PAGE AS MESSY AS YOU CAN

ALFIE'S CAKE IN A MUG RECIPE...

WATCH ALFIE IN ACTION

INGREDIENTS

4 TBSP SELF-RAISING FLOUR

2 TBSP COCOA POWDER

4 TBSP CASTER SUGAR

3 TBSP MILK

1 MEDIUM EGG

3 TBSP VEGETABLE/ SUNFLOWER OIL

A FEW DROPS VANILLA ESSENCE (IF YOU'RE FEELING POSH)

2 TBSP CHOCOLATE CHIPS

METHOD

FIND A MUG. MAKE SURE IT'S A BIG ONE OTHERWISE IT'LL OVERFLOW IN THE MICROWAVE. PLUS WE ALL LIKE A BIG CAKE

THEN GET ALL THE INGREDIENTS OUT THE CUPBOARD AND READY. ADD THE FLOUR, COCOA POWDER AND SUGAR TO THE MUG AND MIX INTO A CHOCOLATY PASTE. ADD THE EGG AND GIVE IT A GOOD MIX; THEN ADD EVERYTHING ELSE - SO THE MILK, VEGETABLE OIL AND THE VANILLA ESSENCE - BUT NOT THE CHOCOLATE CHIPS! ONCE YOU HAVE EVERYTHING IN THE MUG AND IT'S LOOKING SMOOTH AND DELICIOUS ADD THE CHOCOLATE CHIPS.

PLACE YOUR LOVELY MUG IN THE MIDDLE OF THE MICROWAVE AND COOK ON THE HIGHEST SETTING FOR 4-5 MINUTES. KEEP AN EYE ON IT THROUGH THE WINDOW AS IT MIGHT OVERFLOW.

WAIT FOR THE 'DING'. THEN SIT DOWN AND EAT!

REMEMBER TO DRINK LOTS OF WATER TODAY. STAY HYDRATED :)

WRITE WHATEVER'S ON YOUR MIND

...WITHOUT STOPPING UNTIL YOU GET TO THE END OF THE PAGE

DRAW YOUR OWN TIME MACHINE

Past

To when I painted my black boots pink £20

WHEN YOU SEE THIS PAGE FILL IT IN WITH WHATEVER YOU WANT!

A TEAR-OFF LETTER

WRITE SOMEONE YOU KNOW A LETTER ON THIS
PIECE OF PAPER, TEAR IT OFF AND SEND IT TO THEM

TEAR HERE

DOT
TO
DOT!

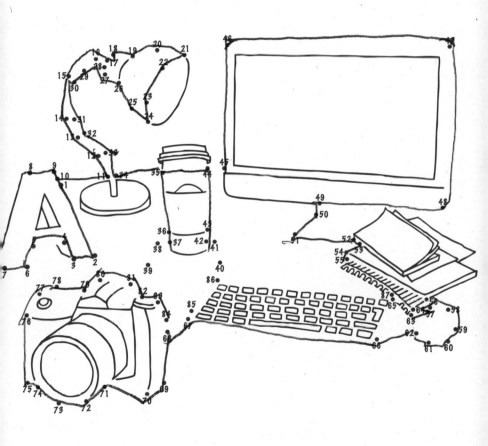

BURY THIS BOOK UNDERGROUND

(FOR ONE NIGHT, DIG IT UP AND SIGN THIS PAGE ONCE YOU'VE DONE SO.)

DATE: _____

SIGN HERE: _____

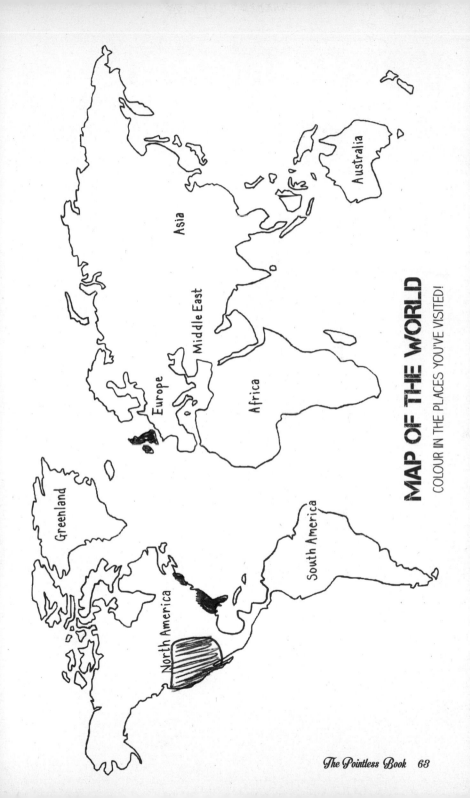

MAP OF THE WORLD
COLOUR IN THE PLACES YOU'VE VISITED!

Asia

Australia

Middle East

Europe

Africa

Greenland

North America

South America

MY LIFE AMBITIONS...

IN MY LIFE I WOULD LIKE TO...

1.

2.

3.

4.

5.

6.

PAPER AIRPLANE COMPETITION

RIP OUT THIS PAGE AND MAKE A PAPER AIRPLANE.

TEAR OUT

② FOLD

FOLD ②

FOLD ①

TEAR OUT

③ FOLD

③ FOLD

⑤ FOLD

⑤ FOLD

④ FOLD

FIVE YOGA POSITIONS TO LEARN...

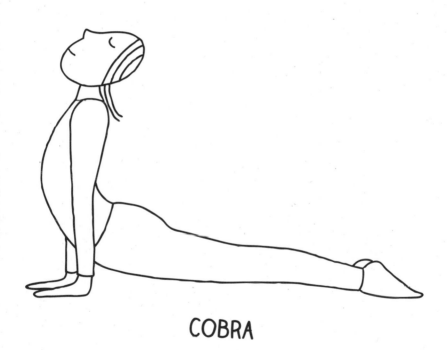

COBRA

FIVE YOGA POSITIONS TO LEARN...

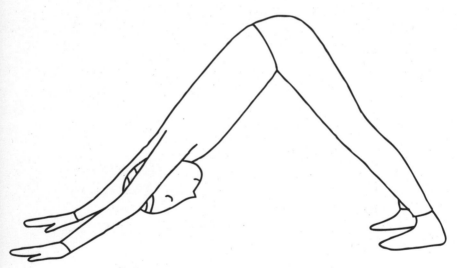

DOWNWARD-FACING DOG

WATCH ALFIE IN ACTION

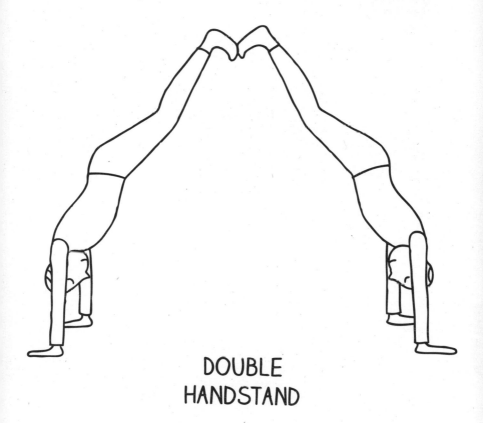

DOUBLE
HANDSTAND

FIVE YOGA POSITIONS TO LEARN...

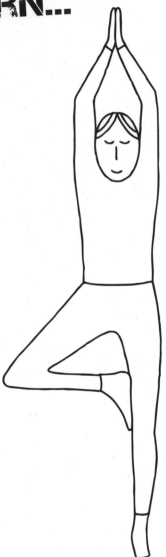

TREE

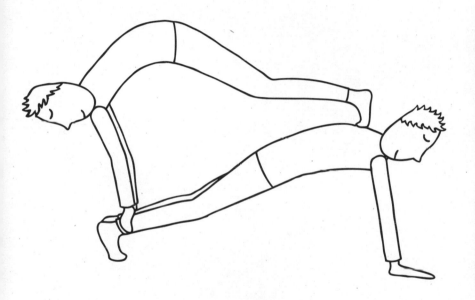

DOUBLE
TRIANGLE

GO TO PAGE 97

GO TO PAGE 97

MESSAGE IN A BOOK...

WRITE A MESSAGE ON THIS PAGE, RIP IT OUT AND SNEAK IT
INTO ANOTHER BOOK IN SCHOOL OR IN THE LIBRARY

TEAR HERE

This book (Page) belongs to YOU!

Please or instagram

IF YOU'RE LUCKY ENOUGH TO FIND THIS PAGE TWEET
#THEPOINTLESSBOOK

The Pointless Book   73

#THEPOINTLESSBOOK

DRAW A FINGER SELFIE...

PLACE A FINGER IN ONE OF THE SPACES BELOW AND DRAW A FACE, A BEARD, A CRAZY MOUSTACHE, WHATEVER YOU LIKE AND THERE YOU GO - YOU HAVE A FINGER SELFIE! SHARE YOUR FINGER SELFIES BY POSTING WITH #PBFINGERSELFIE

PLACES I'D LIKE TO TRAVEL TO...

PLAY SQUARES...

...WITH A FRIEND. TAKE TURNS MAKING A LINE JOINING TWO DOTS BUT TRY TO PREVENT THE OTHER PLAYER FROM MAKING A SQUARE. FILL THE DOTS WITH SQUARES AND THE PERSON WITH THE MOST WINS!

MY FAVOURITE CHILDHOOD MEMORY IS...

SEE ALFIE'S MEMORY

Painting my books Pink!

GRAFFITI THIS WALL

TURN THIS PAGE WITH YOUR ELBOW →

WHAT IS THE LAST THING YOU DO BEFORE YOU FALL ASLEEP AND WHY?

TURN THIS PAGE WITH YOUR EAR

FLICK SOME PAINT ON THIS PAGE

BASKETBALL CHALLENGE

CRUMPLE UP THIS PAGE AND THROW PAPER IN A BASKET-BIN

FINISH OFF THE PICTURE...

One way

Times Square

Central Park

NOT TO DO LIST...

WRITE DOWN FIVE THINGS YOU'D LIKE TO AVOID DOING TODAY:

1. Crying

2. hitting

3. being greedy

4. getting teased

5. being sad

WRITE DOWN A SECRET...

ROAD TRIP!

First one to see a:...

RED CAR ☐

SERVICE STATION ☐

CROW ☐

TYRE ON THE SIDE OF THE ROAD ☐

GIRL WITH BLONDE HAIR ☐

GUY WEARING A BLUE T-SHIRT ☐

HITCHHIKER ☐

SEAGULL ☐

ROAD KILL ☐

BURGER VAN ☐

THE HEADBAND CHALLENGE

Rip out and write down the name of a famous person on the strips below. You and a mate lick and stick it on your head (don't look!) and each person asks a 'yes' or 'no' question in order to guess who their person is.

TEAR HERE

TEAR HERE

TEAR HERE

TEAR HERE

TEAR HERE

TEAR HERE

TEAR HERE

DO SOMETHING YOU'VE NEVER DONE BEFORE AND WRITE IT DOWN HERE.

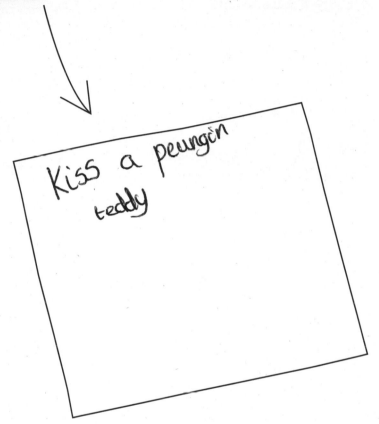

Kiss a peungin
teddy

DRAW YOUR DAY IN A STORYBOARD

DRAW HERE

WRITE HERE

DATE: __ / __ / __

PASS THIS BOOK...

...WITH A GROUP OF FRIENDS
PASS THE BOOK UNDER YOUR
CHIN, WHOEVER DROPS IT IS OUT!

Done!

CHALLENGE TIME

OK, LET'S SEE HOW LONG YOU CAN BE SILENT FOR...

ATTEMPT 1: _____

ATTEMPT 2: _____

ATTEMPT 3: _____

ATTEMPT 4: _____

ATTEMPT 5: _____

PERSONAL BEST: _____

PRESS SOME FLOWERS...

...BETWEEN THESE PAGES

PAINT A PICTURE USING ONLY YOUR FINGERS...

LOVE LETTER...

...TEAR THIS PAGE OUT AND WRITE SOMEONE A LOVE LETTER

TEAR HERE

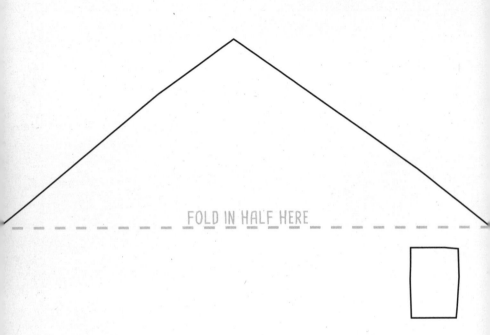

FOLD IN HALF HERE

PHONE BINGO!

Play Phone Bingo with a friend (or group of friends). Call a random person in your contacts and each player has to get the selected list of words below into the conversation, cross them off, then shout 'Phone Bingo!'

GIRAFFE

SHOELACE

CHICKEN WING

UNICYCLE

EAR WAX

USE YOUR OLD NAIL VARNISH TO PAINT THIS PAGE

WHEN YOU SEE THIS PAGE FILL IT IN WITH WHATEVER YOU WANT!

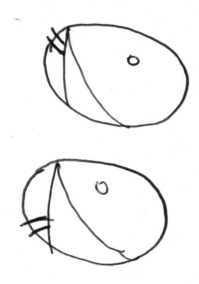

WRITE DOWN WHATEVER YOU DID ON THE PREVIOUS PAGE AND THE REASON WHY YOU DID IT

I drew eyes because my teddy has cute eyes!

MUSIC MAKER!

WRITE A SELECTION OF LYRICS FROM YOUR TOP
FIVE FAVOURITE SONGS AND MAKE UP A NEW SONG:

HEAD, BODY AND TAILS

WITH A GROUP OF FRIENDS, TAKE IT IN TURN TO DRAW THE PARTS OF A PERSON ON THE PAGE BELOW. BEGIN WITH THE HEAD, FOLD THE PAGE AND PASS TO WHOEVER IS ON YOUR RIGHT. ONCE YOU'VE COMPLETED THE HEAD, SHOULDERS, BODY, LEGS AND FEET, OPEN IT UP TO REVEAL YOUR CREATION!

HEAD

TEAR HERE

SHOULDERS

BODY

LEGS

FEET

ANAGRAM PAGE!

Un-scramble the following Pointless anagrams:

GOBLIN TOPLESS

_____

EARN DUVET

_____

MIMES MUTER

_____

HAT PAY SPY

_____

HAPPY HOG ROT

_____

WRITE A POEM...

Roses are Red
Violets are blue
This is a poo poem
just like you

BRAIN TEASERS...

TRY YOUR BEST TO SOLVE THESE:

WHAT TRAVELS AROUND THE WORLD BUT STAYS IN THE CORNER?

_____

WHAT GETS WETTER AND WETTER THE MORE IT DRIES? _____

WHAT CAN YOU CATCH BUT CAN'T THROW?

_rain_____

WHICH WORD IN THE DICTIONARY IS SPELLED INCORRECTLY? _____

YOU CAN HOLD IT WITHOUT USING YOUR ARMS. WHAT IS IT?

_____

NOTES

USE THIS PAGE WHEN YOU NEED SOME PAPER!

POINTLESS PAGE!

WHEN YOU SEE THIS PAGE FILL IT IN WITH WHATEVER YOU WANT!

TURN TO PAGE 15

DESIGN YOUR OWN ALBUM COVER

HAPPY LITTLE PILL

MY JOURNAL THIS WEEK

WRITE DOWN ONE SENTENCE TO DESCRIBE EACH
DAY THIS WEEK.

MONDAY _____

_____

TUESDAY _____

_____

WEDNESDAY _____

_____

THURSDAY _____

_____

FRIDAY _____

_____

SATURDAY _____

_____

SUNDAY _____

_____

CONSEQUENCES...

GAME 1:

(SEE RULES ON PAGE 40)

FOLD HERE

GAME 2:

FOLD HERE

TEAR THE CORNERS OFF THIS PAGE

404 PAGE NOT FOUND

LOL !

HOLE-PUNCH THIS PAGE!

CREATE SOME ART USING A HOLE-PUNCH!

ROCK, PAPER, SCISSORS

SCAN HERE

KEEP SCORE HERE:

PLAYER 1	PLAYER 2

WINNER:

DRAW AROUND YOUR OWN HAND...

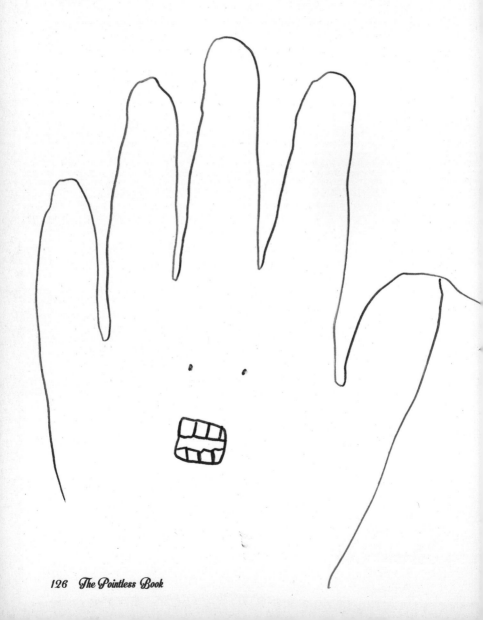

THUMB WARS

KEEP SCORE HERE:

PLAYER 1	PLAYER 2

 **WINNER:** _____

PEOPLE WATCHING PAGE...

TICK WHEN YOU SEE:

☐ SOMEONE WEARING FLIP-FLOPS

☐ SOMEONE RIDING A SKATEBOARD

☐ TOO MUCH PDA (PUBLIC DISPLAY OF AFFECTION)

☐ SOMEONE WEARING A BANDANA

☐ SOMEONE RUNNING FOR A BUS

☐ A TREE TALLER THAN YOUR HOUSE

TURN THIS PAGE WITH YOUR NOSE

TURN TO PAGE 190

DOODLE

FILL THIS PAGE WITH DOODLES

HEAD TENNIS

LOOK RIGHT!

$$\longrightarrow$$

LOOK LEFT!

DRAW YOUR WEEK IN A STORYBOARD

DRAW HERE

WRITE HERE

DATE: _____ / /

F-TEST!

COUNT EVERY "F" IN THE FOLLOWING TEXT

FUNNY FRIENDS ARE
THE RESULT OF YEARS
OF SCIENTIFIC STUDY
COMBINED WITH THE
EXPERIENCE OF YEARS...

2

WRITE WHAT YOU DID TODAY

opened presents
!
'

25th Dec

WHAT'S THE FIRST THING YOU DO IN THE MORNING AND WHY?

go on my phone
cuz i do

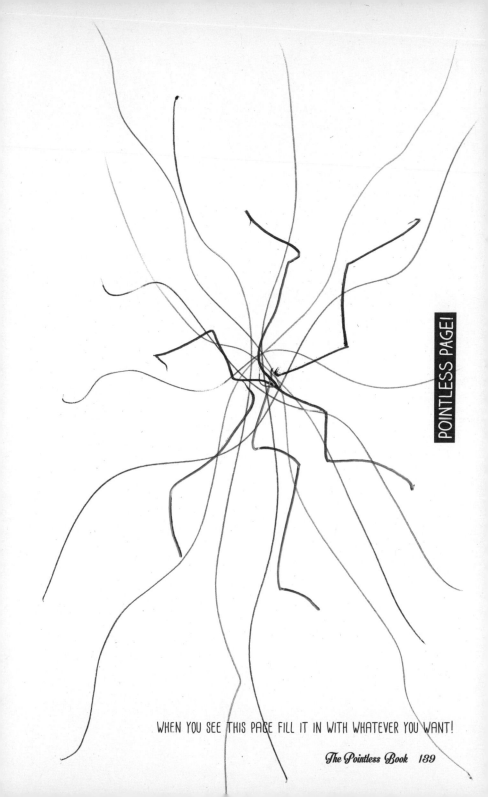

POINTLESS PAGE!

WHEN YOU SEE THIS PAGE FILL IT IN WITH WHATEVER YOU WANT!

RANDOM TWEET!

WHENEVER YOU OPEN
THE BOOK OR PASS
THIS PAGE YOU HAVE TO
TWEET SOMETHING WITH

#THEPOINTLESSBOOK

DRAW A 'SELFIE'

TIME CAPSULE

PUT SOMETHING BETWEEN THESE TWO PAGES
AND GLUE THEM TOGETHER. WRITE A DATE ON
THE NEXT PAGE AND DO NOT OPEN UNTIL THEN.

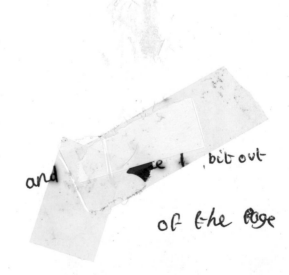

and ⟶ , bit out

of the page

The stuff I had in
my Lush box

25th December

DO NOT OPEN THIS CAPSULE UNTIL

25/12/05

DRAW YOUR PET

WITH A FRIEND SEE HOW LONG YOU CAN DIP A BISCUIT IN YOUR CUP OF TEA BEFORE IT BREAKS OFF

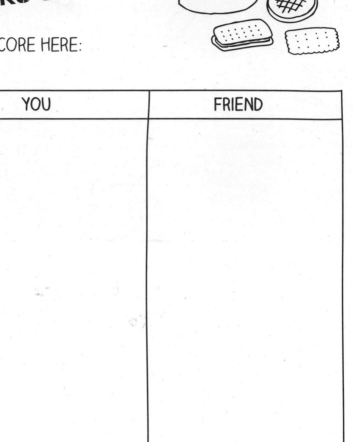

KEEP SCORE HERE:

YOU	FRIEND

WRITE DOWN SOME FUNNY OVERHEARD CONVERSATIONS...

oh hey!

ho

its of to work we go

hey ho

DRAW A LANDMARK...

...FROM A PLACE YOU WOULD LIKE TO VISIT

Brighton peir

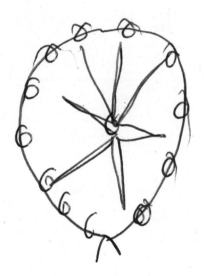

CRAZY COCKTAIL

MAKE THE WEIRDEST COCKTAIL POSSIBLE! JOT DOWN WHAT YOU'VE PUT IN IT (KETCHUP, MUSTARD...) AND RATE HOW IT TASTED OUT OF 10.

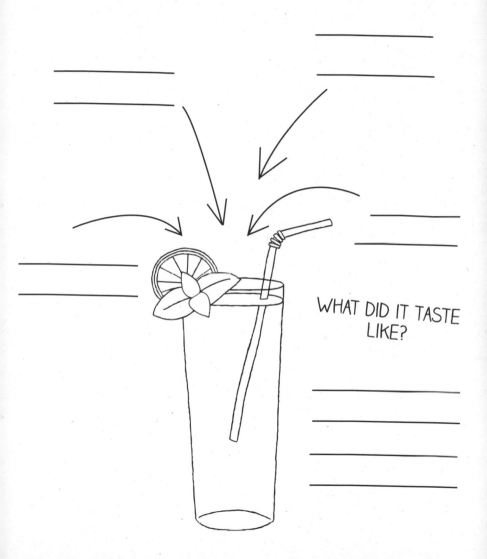

WHAT DID IT TASTE LIKE?

MAKE A FACE USING MAGAZINE CUT-OUTS...

MAKE A SMOOTHIE FROM WHATEVER YOU HAVE IN THE FRIDGE...

INGREDIENTS:

_____

_____

_____

_____

_____

_____

_____

_____

_____   WHAT DID IT
                                              TASTE LIKE?
_____

_____

_____

_____

_____

_____

_____

_____

LIST YOUR TOP FIVE FILMS

1. Elf

2. Zalfie the movie

3. Tanya the movie

4. narcus the movie

5. ↑ PIƷ↑

MY FIRST...

1. WORD

2. FRIEND *Leah*

3. PET *Fudge*

4. KISS *EWWW*

5. FEAR *??*

6. JOB *none*

7. PHONE *Samsung 1*

STICK A PHOTO HERE OF WHEN YOU WERE YOUNG

DRAW WHAT YOU'D LIKE TO BE
WHEN YOU'RE OLDER

ABC

teacher

ON THE BOARD BELOW WRITE DOWN THE NAME OF FOUR PEOPLE (TWO YOU LIKE, TWO YOU DISLIKE), FOUR COUNTRIES, AND FOUR RANDOM NUMBERS. GRAB A PEN AND TAP INSIDE THE BOX UNTIL A NOMINATED PLAYER SAYS 'STOP!' COUNT THE DOTS AND, BEGINNING WITH 'M', USE THIS NUMBER TO CROSS OFF THE ANSWERS SURROUNDING THE BOX, CROSSING OFF AN ANSWER EVERY TIME YOU GET TO YOUR NUMBER. THE GAME IS COMPLETE WHEN ONE ANSWER REMAINS IN EACH PANEL...

MASH

MANSION   APARTMENT   SHED   HOUSE

NAMES

COUNTRIES

KIDS

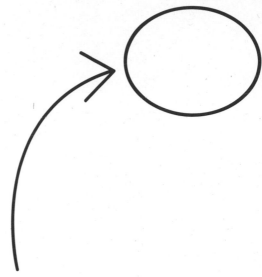

STICK CHEWING GUM
HERE AND FOLD THE CORNER

WHAT DID I DO ON THIS DAY...?

NEW YEAR'S DAY _____

_____

_____

EASTER MONDAY _____

_____

_____

ST PATRICK'S DAY _____

_____

_____

MIDSUMMER'S DAY _____

_____

_____

AUGUST BANK HOLIDAY _____

_____

_____

WHO WOULD YOU INVITE TO YOUR DREAM DINNER PARTY?

Zalfie ♡
Narcus ♡
Janya ♡

Xxx

WOULD YOU RATHER...

1) Be boiling hot or freezing cold?

2) Have your computer memory wiped or have your past and future web browsing history available to everyone?

3) Drink a cup of public swimming pool water or sea water?

4) Hiccup for the rest of your life or feel like you have to sneeze but can't for the rest of your life?

5) Listen to one song for the rest of your life or never listen to the same song twice?

6) Not be able to use the internet or not be able to listen to music?

SNOG, MARRY, AVOID...

SNOG ☐

MARRY ☐

AVOID ☐

_____

SNOG ☐

MARRY ☐

AVOID ☐

_____

SNOG ☐

MARRY ☐

AVOID ☐

_____

DESCRIBE YOURSELF IN FIVE WORDS...

Awesome
Epic
beast
Cool
Swag

USE THIS PAGE
WHEN YOU
DESPERATELY NEED
TOILET PAPER

...DON'T FORGET TO FLUSH...

TURN THIS PAGE WITH YOUR TOE

$\longrightarrow$

POINTLESS PAGE!

TELL A STRANGER A JOKE

SEE ALFIE'S JOKE

DID THEY:

1. LAUGH
2. CRY
3. VOMIT
4. RUN AWAY

ANAGRAM ANSWERS

GOBLIN TOPLESS

POINTLESS BLOG

EARN DUVET

ADVENTURE

MIMES MUTER

SUMMER TIME

HAT PAY SPY

STAY HAPPY

HAPPY HOG ROT

PHOTOGRAPHY

BRAIN-TEASER ANSWERS

WHAT TRAVELS AROUND THE WORLD BUT STAYS IN THE CORNER?

A POSTAGE STAMP

WHAT GETS WETTER AND WETTER THE MORE IT DRIES?

A TOWEL

WHAT CAN YOU CATCH BUT CAN'T THROW?

A COLD

WHICH WORD IN THE DICTIONARY IS SPELLED INCORRECTLY?

INCORRECTLY

YOU CAN HOLD IT WITHOUT USING YOUR ARMS. WHAT IS IT?

YOUR BREATH

WRITE FIVE THINGS YOU LIKE BEST ABOUT YOURSELF AND WHY...

1. _____
_____
_____
_____

2. _____
_____
_____
_____

3. _____
_____
_____
_____

4. _____
_____
_____
_____

5. _____
_____
_____
_____

SPARE PAPER...

...USE THIS PAGE WHEN YOU NEED SOME PAPER

CREATE SOME ART HERE WITH THE HOLES FROM THE HOLE-PUNCH PAGE!

(FROM PAGE 123)

BASKETBALL CHALLENGE

CRUMPLE UP THIS PAGE AND THROW PAPER IN A BASKET · BIN

TOP FIVE THINGS...

...THAT MAKE YOU WANT TO VOMIT.

1. _____

2. _____

3. _____

4. _____

5. _____

CUT OUT NEWSPAPER HEADLINES...

...AND MAKE A STORY HERE!

WRITE A COMPLIMENT...

...RIP OUT THIS PAGE AND GIVE IT TO A STRANGER.

TEAR HERE

FILL THIS PAGE

WITH THINGS YOU LOVE...

SPOT THE DIFFERENCE
ANSWERS...

WORD SEARCH ANSWERS...

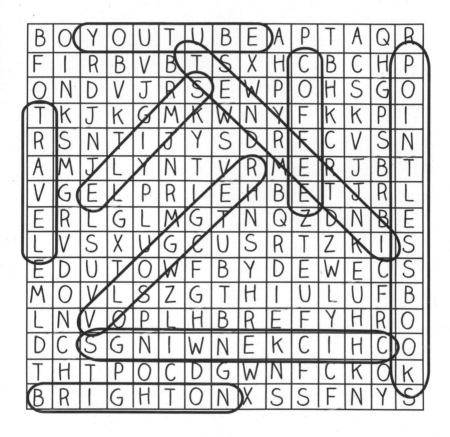

B	O	Y	O	U	T	U	B	E	A	P	T	A	Q	R
F	I	R	B	V	B	T	S	X	H	C	B	C	H	P
O	N	D	V	J	R	S	E	W	P	O	H	S	G	O
T	K	J	K	G	M	K	W	N	Y	F	K	K	P	I
R	S	N	T	I	J	Y	S	D	R	F	C	V	S	N
A	M	J	L	Y	N	T	V	R	M	E	R	J	B	T
V	G	E	L	P	R	I	E	H	B	E	T	R	R	L
E	R	L	G	L	M	G	T	N	Q	Z	D	N	B	E
L	V	S	X	U	G	C	U	S	R	T	Z	K	I	S
E	D	U	T	O	W	F	B	Y	D	E	W	E	C	S
M	O	V	L	S	Z	G	T	H	I	U	L	U	F	B
L	N	V	O	P	L	H	B	R	E	F	Y	H	R	O
D	C	S	G	N	I	W	N	E	K	C	I	H	C	O
T	H	T	P	O	C	D	G	W	N	F	C	K	O	K
B	R	I	G	H	T	O	N	X	S	S	F	N	Y	S

YOUTUBE   SMILE   COFFEE

VLOGGER   BRIGHTON   INTERNET

POINTLESS BOOK   TRAVEL   CHICKEN WINGS

BALANCE THE BOOK ON YOUR HEAD CHALLENGE!

INSTRUCTIONS:

1. CLOSE YOUR POINTLESS BOOK (NOT NOW - WAIT UNTIL YOU'VE READ ALL OF THE INSTRUCTIONS FIRST!).

2. STAND IN AN OPEN SPACE AND MAKE SURE THERE AREN'T ANY OBSTACLES IN YOUR WAY.

3. PLACE THE BOOK ON THE MIDDLE OF YOUR HEAD AND TAKE A STEP FORWARD.

HOW MANY STEPS CAN YOU TAKE?

TWEET YOUR BEST TIME TO #THEPOINTLESSBOOK

TURN TO PAGE 34

DRAW THESE HYBRID ANIMALS: A ZEDONKEY, A GORILLAROO, A CABBIT AND A FROGODILE!

A GEEP

CELEBRITY FISH NAME GAME

FILL THESE PAGES WITH AS MANY CELEBRITY FISH NAMES YOU AND YOUR FRIENDS CAN THINK OF! HERE ARE A FEW TO START YOU OFF:

TUNA TURNER

MUSSEL CROWE

CALAMARI DIAZ

The Pointless Book* 187

GIVE THIS BOOK TO A FRIEND...

...AND ASK THEM TO DESCRIBE YOU IN THREE WORDS:

DOODLE TIME!

TURN TO PAGE 130

←

SUGGEST MORE WAYS THIS BOOK CAN BE POINTLESS. FILL OUT THE BOXES BELOW AND SEND IT TO THE ADDRESS OVERLEAF...

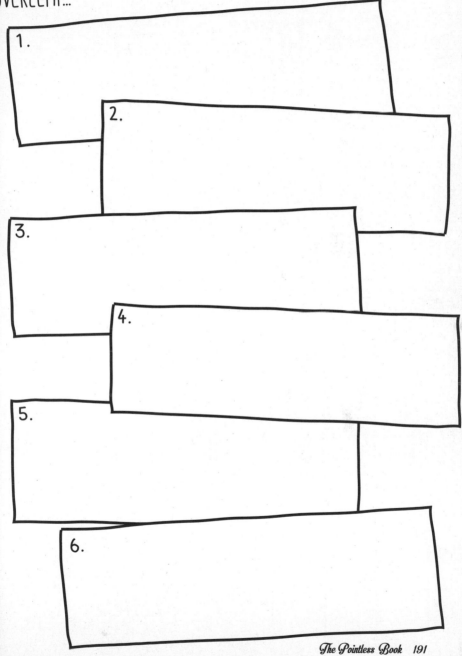

1.

2.

3.

4.

5.

6.

BLINK PUBLISHING

DEEPDENE LODGE

DEEPDENE AVENUE

DORKING, RH5 4AT,

UNITED KINGDOM